THE GREAT STORM
IN CANTERBURY
25 YEARS ON

PAUL CRAMPTON

First published 2012

The History Press
The Mill, Brimscombe Port
Stroud, Gloucestershire, GL5 2QG
www.thehistorypress.co.uk

British Library Cataloguing in Publication Data.
A catalogue record for this book is available from the British Library.

ISBN 978 0 7524 6752 8

Typesetting and origination by The History Press
Manufacturing managed by Jellyfish Print Solutions Ltd
Printed in India.

CONTENTS

Fortunately, many more trees were damaged than destroyed in the Great Storm. Many deciduous trees in particular recovered well, especially those traditionally subject to coppicing. Here, the author's grandfather has been pressed into service, clearing the fallen branches from a weeping willow tree in the author's parents' back garden.

Unlike trees, buildings cannot repair themselves. In any case, far smaller outbuildings, such as garages and greenhouses, were lost than were the larger houses and shops, which was just as well! Here, Peter Docherty takes a break while his grandson, Neil Burton, helps stack up the remains of his garage.

ACKNOWLEDGEMENTS

While I took the vast majority of the photographs reproduced in this book, I want to extend my appreciation to the few other people whose work also appears here: to Sarah Crampton, for the picture of me up a ladder, and to Ken Wood for the traction engine quartet.

Above: A series of farm outbuildings at Hillborough, on the outskirts of Herne Bay, where the Great Storm caused much damage. This area has since been redeveloped for housing.

Left: A massive London plane tree has been ripped from the ground along The Causeway, in one of a series of pictures taken on 16th October 1987. Note the uprooted telephone ducting and cables, rendering a number of local telephones useless, including the author's!

FOREWORD

Many years ago, I approached the writer and broadcaster John Arlott to ask whether he would kindly write the foreword to my book 100 *Years of Sturry Cricket*. He kindly agreed and wrote the following: 'The compliment of being asked to write the foreword to another man's book is always pleasant.'

The opportunity to write an introduction to Paul's follow-up book on the 1987 Hurricane – *The Great Storm of 1987 in Canterbury: 25 Years On* – is also a pleasant thing for me to do. The hurricane, or Great Storm, occurred on the night of 15/16th October 1987 and affected much of Southern England. Those who lived through it will remember how terrifying it was and I clearly recall the sound of the glass in my greenhouse exploding. I drove through Wincheap at around 9 a.m. in the morning on my way to work (probably a foolish thing to do considering the state of the roads) and remember the large chimneystack on the Hop Poles public house leaning in a rather precarious position.

We are indebted to Paul for risking life and limb to take photographs of the local area on the morning of the 16th October as they are a unique record of that event: the worst storm in England since 1703. With Paul's great knowledge of Canterbury, and his thorough research, I can highly recommend this book, updated with new material and published in full-colour. I am sure it will appeal to both local people who lived through this frightening event and to the younger generation who will hopefully never experience such an occasion.

Derek Butler

A small coach-house off Tower Way, in Canterbury, which was badly damaged in the Great Storm. It is seen here in the summer of 1988, shortly after the precariously remaining roof had suddenly collapsed.

INTRODUCTION

In the south-east of England, most of us remember where we were when the Great Storm of 1987 was at its height: the vast majority of us were in bed! Reassured by the bespectacled BBC weatherman Michael Fish, we all went to bed on the night of 15th/16th October secure in the knowledge that there would be no hurricane, and that those few voices of doom were exaggerating at best. There may have been no hurricane, in the strictest definition, but it jolly well felt like one.

I awoke in the small hours of Friday, 16th October 1987 to an unfamiliar roaring sound outside. At the time, I lived quite close to the railway line in the St Stephen's suburb of Canterbury, so my first thought was that the roaring sound was a train passing by. However, the noise persisted, along with a strange tinkling, almost as if glass were breaking. I got out of bed and pulled the curtains open to reveal a scene blurred by rain. It was then that I realised all was not well. I quickly established that the tinkling sound was coming from next door's greenhouse, as each pane smashed, sending shards of glass flying into the side wall of my garage. I clearly wouldn't be going outside in a hurry!

Going back to bed, I tried to return to sleep, but this was impossible. I sat up and clicked on the bedside lamp: nothing. The power was out; a cable must be down; perhaps many cables! It was then that I heard the sound of my TV aerial snapping off and sliding down the roof immediately above me. I wouldn't be able to watch a Michael Fish weather forecast now, even if I wanted to! When the massive gable end of Holter's Mill, at the end of my back lane, came crashing to the ground, I realised that lives were in danger. I reached for the bedroom telephone: I had a dialling tone, but it was still quite early in the morning. No need to alarm my family unnecessarily, I reasoned. Perhaps this hurricane was confined to Canterbury.

As the frame of next door's greenhouse lifted up, following its erstwhile glazing into my back garden, I could wait no longer: I had to establish that my loved ones were alright. I dialled my parents' number in Here Bay, but could not get through. I then rang my girlfriend, Sarah, who lived about a mile away. The number connected, rang out, and she answered almost straight away. She was fine, although her neighbour's rabbit hutch, complete with dazed occupant, had just landed in her back garden. The distressed young owner's father, dressed in a hastily donned pink tracksuit, had just rushed through the broken fence and rescued the poor rabbit, who seemed none the worse for his unexpected flight!

My battery-operated transistor radio soon confirmed that the whole of the south-east of England was experiencing the 'hurricane' that had been so casually dismissed only hours before. Having washed and dressed, I went downstairs to re-try my parents' number, again to no avail. Luckily, the phone service was erratic, and I finally got through on my third attempt. They were OK, as were my grandparents next door to them, but it sounded as if things on the Kent coast were even worse. My family had already heard tales of coastal flooding and caravans being overturned at Reculver.

By about 7.30 a.m., I decided that I would try to get to work. I walked to work in Canterbury at the time, varying my duties for BT between Telephone House and Becket House. One of my keenest hobbies at the time was photography. Having returned to living in the city of my birth, I had been recording some of the changes and developments that had taken place in Canterbury. I had also been taking many photographs during those much-anticipated Sunday-morning country walks with my grandfather and brother. Many pictures from the latter would soon be serving me very well, but I had no idea that this would be the case on the morning of 16th October 1987.

The idea of capturing some of the scenes of devastation in Canterbury en-route to work quickly became the motivating factor for leaving home, and so I set off, with a fresh roll of thirty-six exposures in my trusty OM10 and a spare roll in my jacket pocket. By now it was 8 a.m., and the wind had died down considerably and there were few cars about on the branch-strewn streets. I took my first batch of photographs in The Causeway, where vast Victorian-era London plane trees had been ripped from the ground and thrown across roads and pavements. The rest of my walk to work that day is told in the dramatic photos on the pages that follow.

On my arrival at work, I discovered that the power was out at Telephone House, and the phones barely worked, so we were given lukewarm coffee, praised for having made the effort to get in (where so many hadn't), and sent home again. Great, I thought, another opportunity for photographs. I decided not to take any pictures of private houses that had been damaged. Yes, they would have been dramatic, but there was more than enough to see and record without needing to capitalise on other people's distress.

That afternoon I met up with Sarah, and we went to her parents' house in Rough Common: a village on the high ground to the west of Canterbury. With their permission, I relaxed my self-imposed censorship and proceeded to take pictures of the terrible damage we found in St Michael's Close. The exposed gable end of their bungalow had taken the full brunt of the storm. All the tiles along the roof edge at that end of the bungalow had crashed to the ground or been dislodged. Worst of all, the entire detached garage had collapsed, with Peter's brand new car inside! I volunteered to mount a ladder (leant against the aforementioned dodgy gable end) to try and bring down those dislodged tiles that were still hanging precariously, and was partially successful in the endeavour.

In the weeks that followed, I continued to take photographs on those Sunday morning walks, including many of damaged buildings and toppled trees. It gradually occurred to me that I was recording scenes of devastation where I had already taken an earlier pre-Great Storm photo. And so I began putting together some 'before' and 'after' pictures.

It is hard to believe that twenty-five years have now elapsed since that frightening morning, and it wasn't until I pitched the idea of an anniversary book (this time in colour) to The History Press, that the sheer amount of water that had passed beneath the proverbial bridge since then really came home to me.

All of the photographs that appeared in the 1988 book are reproduced here in colour, with the addition of many previously unpublished views taken at the time. However, I have decided to omit most of the 'aftermath' pictures in order to concentrate on the impact of the Great Storm itself. Instead, the aftermath is represented by the so-called 'hurricane carvings' that appeared on Miller's Field in the months that followed the storm. By contrast, the number of pictures in chapter two, 'The Canterbury District', have been reduced, omitting similar views of toppled trees that appeared in the original black-and-white book. The many pictures that did make it through, however, are reproduced here, in colour, for the first time.

Paul Crampton, 2012

1

THE CITY OF CANTERBURY

The magnificent Harbledown cedar of Lebanon tree, as seen from Westgate Court Avenue in the summer of 1986. Originally, this specimen tree is likely to have been planted as part of a Capability Brown-style landscape garden associated with a large house called The Hermitage, which fronted Summer Hill in Harbledown.

The Harbledown cedar, from the footbridge over the bypass, in July 1986. This tree once stood on the edge of Duke's Meadow, but when the Harbledown bypass cut a vast swathe through this once much-loved public open space, in the mid-1970s, the tree was preserved by constructing a special stone-lined plinth around its roots.

Sadly, the cedar tree was badly damaged in the Great Storm, so much so that its removal was deemed the only practical solution. The freshly sawn stump is pictured here, with the footbridge in the distance. Cedar of Lebanon trees cannot re-grow from the base and roots, as can many English broad-leaf species, so this meant the tree's demise.

Another view from the bridge over the bypass, this time on 8th November 1987, shortly after the remains of the cedar had been cleared away. The repair of the damage caused to an adjacent property, attributed to a severed limb from the tree, can clearly be seen.

The final photograph in this sequence dates from October 2011, and the bypass bridge is once again the vantage point used. A replacement cedar of Lebanon tree was planted on the same plinth in 1988, and this slow-growing specimen can just be seen amongst the Sycamore scrub that has recently been allowed to flourish along this part of the bypass cutting.

By 8 a.m. on 16th October 1987 the storm has died down, but the wind is still strong enough to bend the surviving trees along The Causeway.

This determined woman in The Causeway is not going to allow these toppled London plane trees to impede her progress, even if it means scrambling underneath them.

The fallen plane trees, as seen from the other side, on the morning of 16th October. The autumnal sun, rising from behind the Cathedrals' Bell Harry Tower, begins to illuminate the scene.

The Causeway in October 2011, just as the first leaves of autumn are beginning to fall. Note the replacement tree saplings (centre left), which are making good progress.

The first of four views taken by Ken Wood in the immediate aftermath of the Great Storm. A tree has fallen against the wall of St Mildred's churchyard, and work is beginning on the removal of some of its heavier branches.

With the branches cut off, a JCB was employed to drag the heavy tree trunk up the slope, but the work proved too arduous for it. In the end, a preserved steam traction engine was pressed into service and managed the task with no problem whatsoever.

The ancient and the modern, or the victor and the vanquished, pose for the camera on the incoming carriageway of the Rheims Way, which had been closed during the recovery operations.

The last of Ken's quartet is a fine view of the traction engine, at rest, during the recovery task. Note the wooden choc against the back wheels for bracing purposes. At the time, this 1931 machine, named 'Rob Roy' and with registration number OU 9309, was part of The Royal Museum Collection at Sarre, in Kent.

Miller's Field is a triangular island, bordered on every side by the River Stour. This view from North Lane, looking towards Pound Lane, dates from April 1987. The trunks of some fourteen trees can be counted.

A scene of utter devastation across Miller's Field, at lunchtime on 16th October 1987. Note that only one tree remains standing in this view taken from The Causeway.

Miller's Field in April 1988, captured from North Lane in exactly the same spot as the view on the opposite page. The legacy of the Great Storm can clearly be seen, and only seven trees can now be counted.

This photograph from October 2011 shows the replacement saplings alongside the more mature survivors of the Great Storm. The London plane tree was the dominant species chosen to reflect those examples that were lost.

The collapsed gable end of Holters Warehouse, St Stephen's Mill, taken from outside the author's garage in Holters Lane at about 8 a.m. on 16th October 1987.

Another view of the storm-damaged mill, seen from across the railway approaches to Canterbury West Station. Note that sections of the building's roof are strewn alongside the railway line.

A close-up of Holters Mill in August 1998, shortly after it had closed prior to residential redevelopment. Note the different coloured brickwork in the gable end, clearly denoting the sections of the building that had to be rebuilt following storm damage.

A current view of the former warehouse in October 2011, from Holters Lane. This is now an exclusive gated community and it was not possible for me to get any closer for a more accurate 'now' photograph.

The morning of 16th October 1987, and a fallen London plane tree on The Causeway has distorted one of Canterbury's classic 'swan-neck' street lamps. Part of the pavement has also been lifted as a result.

The clearing-up process on The Causeway began almost straight away, in an effort to open the thoroughfare to traffic once more. Here, a JCB clears tree branches from the road surface.

Similar clear-up operations in St Stephen's Road, on the afternoon of 16th October 1987. Flooding in certain parts of Canterbury occurred in the immediate aftermath of the Great Storm, although worse was to follow that winter.

The Causeway at the end of October 1987, with traffic now flowing as per usual. However, the distorted street lamp has yet to be removed, and bollards warn passers-by of the potential hazard. Note the tree behind, set at a crazy angle following the affects of the Great Storm.

The ancient tower to St Dunstan's Church in Canterbury, with its wind-distorted weathervane hanging over the parapet in a dangerous manner.

A portion of the same weathervane lying at the base of the tower; its shape twisted following the fall. The tall, exposed church tower would have been severely buffeted by the Great Storm, and the weathervane must have put up a valiant fight before finally succumbing to the inevitable.

The Roper Chapel at St Dunstan's Church on 17th October 1987. The Tudor brick and stone-built parapet has clearly given way, causing thousands of pounds worth of damage as a result.

Debris from the collapsed chapel parapet litters the churchyard at St Dunstan's in the aftermath of the Great Storm. The vaults beneath Roper Chapel house the remains of the famous Canterbury Roper family, together with the severed head of Henry VIII's former chancellor and friend, Sir Thomas More, whose daughter Margaret had married into this Catholic Canterbury family.

The lush foliage of this fine row of London plane trees is quite apparent in this view from the glorious summer of 1987. The location is the water-relief channel between Miller's Field and Pound Lane, at the west end of Canterbury.

The morning of 16th October 1987, and most of the trees have been destroyed by the severe winds of the Great Storm. This picture was taken from the small footbridge immediately adjacent to the sluice gates seen in the above view.

January 1988, and the sluice gates are fully opened to deal with severe flooding along the banks of the River Stour throughout Canterbury and its suburbs. Note the vast crater in the foreground, caused by one of the plane tree's roots being ripped out.

A much calmer and warmer looking scene in April 1988. The after-affects of the Great Storm are clear at this location, with far fewer trees now remaining. The sluice gates would have once controlled how much water went to the Hooker's water mill beyond, and how much was sent along the relief channel (right) that bypassed the mill.

The well-known Dane John Mound is framed here by a fine mixture of mature evergreen and deciduous trees in the summer of 1986. The trees are growing out of the slope to the earth ramparts that protect the inside of the city wall at this location, and also support the city wall path that runs along this stretch.

Lunchtime on 16th October 1987, and the many torn limbs from these, by now, severely damaged trees litter the children's playing area in the Dane John, and have all but buried the swings.

A view from the same part of the city wall, but in the opposite direction, looking over the ringroad towards the East Station. Part of the roof to Palmer's wholesale newspaper distribution depot has been torn off. The building was later repaired and is now run by the Scrine Foundation for homeless people in the city.

The low autumn sun does its best to illuminate the fading foliage of the remaining trees in the Dane John during early October 2011. A new play area for children, in the shadow of the mound, is just visible, as are the tents of a popular food fair often held here.

The churchyard to St Mildred's Church in Canterbury; one of the city's ancient Saxon foundations. A large tree has clearly come to grief here. It is resting against its still-upstanding neighbour and their branches have become interlocked.

The same churchyard seen from the Rheims Way in December 1987. Earlier, the fallen tree had been removed by steam traction engine. Note the damaged churchyard wall, which is a result of the tree's collapse and subsequent removal.

Returning to 16th October 1987 and another view of St Mildred's churchyard. This picture was taken from the footpath that links the Rheims Way with Church Lane.

The same view in October 2011, taken from the same spot as the photograph opposite. It is hard to believe that this weeping willow has been planted and reached this level of maturity in the intervening years. In fact, its canopy is so impressive that views of the Cathedral are no longer possible from this location.

This small bridge carries a track from St Stephen's Road to Frank Hooker Field, over a small branch of the River Stour. Debris from fallen tree branches has built up and caused the water level to rise. Such problems were a contributory factor in the floods that followed in the aftermath of the Great Storm.

A view from the same location taken in October 2011. As can be seen elsewhere in the city, the weeping willow has proved to be amongst the most vigorous of species planted on sites devastated by the Great Storm. This little bridge now carries a footpath that links St Stephen's Road into the main city riverside walk network.

The level of the River Stour has reached a dangerous level in this view from January 1988. The location is Solley's Orchard off St Peter's Lane. The riverbank retaining wall on the left has been swept away. It was damaged by fallen trees in the Great Storm then further compromised in the floods that immediately followed.

This photograph from October 2011 shows a much-changed scene. The retaining wall has been repaired and the calm River Stour slips by, reflecting the autumnal sunlight. The houses on the right front onto Mill Lane and Blackfriar's Street.

An East Kent bus was badly damaged in the aftermath of the Great Storm, having collided with trees that had been blown out of true by the high winds. The accident occurred in the Littlebourne Road, while the bus was on the Canterbury to Deal route. Registered PJJ 20S, this ten-year-old Bristol VRT is pictured here at St Stephen's Road Garage. It was subsequently sold for scrap.

The premises of Practical Kitchens Ltd in St Dunstan's Street, Canterbury, following the Great Storm. Note that the closed doors to the yard behind have been completely ripped off their hinges by the high winds blowing through the passage. This building was soon to be demolished for a housing scheme.

An interesting view of the curved embankment of the former Elham Valley Railway line, as it climbs away from the Ashford line and heads towards the suburb of Wincheap (behind the camera). The line closed in 1947, after which many trees took root along the former track bed.

A photograph taken from the same location on the old railway embankment, in March 1988. The fallen trees had not yet been cleared away at this fairly remote location. The edge of the London Road Estate can be seen on the horizon.

A fine panoramic view of the top end of Westgate Gardens, taken from the roof of Telephone House in April 1987. The riverside rows of poplar trees make an impressive spectacle from such a vantage point.

Ken Wood's view of the top end of Westgate Gardens, in the immediate aftermath of the Great Storm. Note the deep tyre marks left by the lorries and tractors employed to remove the many fallen trees.

A view taken from the same precarious vantage point as that on the opposite page, but this time during January 1988, when the flood waters were at their worst. This part of Canterbury was much loved by Thomas Sidney Cooper, who painted a number of his city views from these meadows.

The final view from Telephone House, this one dating from spring 1988. The number of poplar trees lost in the Great Storm is all too evident. Such views would no longer be possible today, as Telephone House was demolished in October 2005 in favour of a housing scheme.

A somewhat obscured and distant view of the Cathedral, as seen from the upper terrace in St Martin's churchyard during the summer of 1986. Bell Harry Tower can be seen through the branches of this magnificent cedar of Lebanon tree.

November 1987, and an almost exactly replicated view dramatically shows how badly damaged the cedar tree is as a result of the Great Storm. However, it was much more fortunate than the Harbledown cedar, at the opposite end of the city, which had to be felled as a result of the damage it had sustained. A number of smaller evergreen trees have also disappeared completely in the intervening weeks.

An interesting panorama taken from the central reservation of the Rheims Way in the late summer of 1987. This, the first section of the city's ringroad and A2 bypass, was opened in June 1963. Note the fine row of poplar trees growing along the bank of the River Stour.

A similar view taken almost exactly one year later, and the riverside poplar trees are no more. Other surviving trees show considerable signs of damage. Down beyond St Peter's roundabout, some of the tannery buildings can just be seen. This huge site has since been redeveloped for housing.

A forlorn-looking Peter Docherty sits amongst the ruins of his garage in St Michael's Close, Rough Common, and consoles himself with a mug of coffee, having just dug his brand new car out of the rubble.

The author risks life and limb atop an old ladder as he attempts to clear away some of the dislodged tiles from Peter Docherty's roof. It was later discovered that the gable end, against which the ladder was leaning, had shifted a few inches inwards as a result of the Great Storm.

Workmen and contractors begin work to clear away all of the fallen trees on The Causeway at lunchtime on 16th October 1987. One of the largest concentrations of clearance workers in the city could be found at this location, due to the fact that the road was completely blocked, as was a much used car park.

The author's grandfather, Tom Vine, cheerfully clears away the many fallen and shredded branches of the weeping willow tree in the author's parents' garden. Despite a battering, the tree survived and quickly recovered from its ordeal.

Roper Road, in the St Dunstan's suburb of Canterbury, in the late autumn of 1986. The original purpose of this picture was to record the BRS depot, which was about to be demolished for a housing scheme. However, the photograph also recorded a row of trees that would soon suffer heavily in the Great Storm.

The same view captured in March 1988, by which time the warehouse had been cleared away and a new housing scheme begun. The loss to the roadside row of trees, as a result of the Great Storm, is also evident.

Castle Street on the morning of 16th October 1987. A tree from the former churchyard of St Mary de Castro has come to grief, blocking the street to all vehicular traffic. Moving such obstacles would soon become a priority in the clearing-up process.

A view from the inside of St Mary de Castro churchyard showing an ancient tree that had come to grief during the night before. Although no trace of the church now exists above ground, a number of gravestones around the perimeter wall of this area can still be seen.

The bottom end of Lower Chantry Lane, in December 1986, with the low winter sun casting deep shadows over the cars in the surface parking area. To the right, the mature trees in the remote burial ground of St Paul's Church stand in their bare, wintry dormancy.

The same location in March 1988 and the car park is as full as before, but the stock of trees along its perimeter with the old churchyard have been significantly reduced. Gone also is the tree (left) in the grounds of St Augustine's Abbey.

The roof of Telephone House has once again become the vantage point for this impressive cityscape, taken in April 1987. The Cathedral stands out well, as do the group of trees just beyond the carriageways of the Rheims Way, to the left.

It required a lot of nerve to climb the steep metal ladder to capture the above view, and I certainly didn't relish the idea of having to do it twice, but I plucked up the courage in April 1988 in order to take the 'after the hurricane' view. The tree loss on the Rheims Way embankment and along the edge of St Mildred's churchyard is all too evident from this lofty perspective.

Frank Hooker Field, off St Stephen's Road, in January 1987, with the threat of a snowy sky looming. A number of bare-leafed trees can be seen between the playing field and the houses fronting St Stephen's Road.

The same location in April 1988. The tall 'specimen' tree has taken a battering but has survived. Sadly, though, the same cannot be said of the old oak tree to the left, which has since disappeared.

This old coach house off Tower Way was badly damaged in the Great Storm. The picture was taken a few weeks after the event, by which time a chestnut-paling fence had been erected to keep people away from the 'dangerous structure'.

Unfortunately, the roof was subject to further collapse before repair work could be started (*see* page 6). This current view, from October 2011, shows that the coach house had to be almost entirely rebuilt from scratch in order to return it to use.

High Street, Canterbury, on the morning of 16th October 1987, and the author's lasting memory is of the persistent noise created by the sheer number of burglar alarms that had been triggered by the high winds during the previous night. The photograph shows a tree that has also been uprooted from the small open space on the site of the lost St Mary Bredman Church, which had been demolished in 1901.

The oldest part of the tannery complex, at the top end of Stour Street, as seen from the top deck of the Rosemary Lane multi-storey car park in late October 1987. Closer examination will show that many hundreds of tiles have been ripped from the tannery roofs by the high winds of the Great Storm. A number of these buildings have recently been demolished.

Another picture taken along the old Elham Valley railway embankment, captured in late April 1987. This particular view has been taken just after the line veered away from the existing Canterbury to Ashford line at Harbledown Junction off Whitehall Road.

A matching photograph, taken in March 1988, and the self-sown trees along the abandoned embankment have clearly been affected by the Great Storm. By contrast, the trees on the higher ridge beyond appear to have been little affected.

A view of Pound Lane, taken from the junction with The Causeway at about 10.30 a.m. on 16th October 1987. The relief channel is just out of sight to the right. Unfortunately, a number of trees have collapsed onto cars belonging to local residents.

A current view of Pound Lane, taken from the same spot in October 2011. The replacement tree saplings, planted between the road and residents' car parking area, seem to be doing well, despite their slow-growing nature.

The third and final panoramic view taken from the roof of Telephone House off St Andrew's Close. This particular photograph shows Bingley Island in April 1987. Being Canterbury's flood plane, this area has never been developed and exists as a nature reserve and occasional grazing area.

A contrasting view of Bingley Island, seen here on a cold winter's day in January 1988. While principally showing the affects of the seriously flooding that month, the photograph also illustrates the trees that had been lost on 16th October 1987.

In the weeks following the October 1987 devastation, it was decided that some form of appropriate memorial to the Great Storm be made. Around the edge of Miller's Field, many mature London plane trees had come to grief, with their large and impressive root balls having been untimely ripped out of the ground.

Rather than clear away these massive tree roots and severed trunks, a decision was made to turn them into wooden carving to commemorate the storm. The pictures on this page, from July 1988, show work-in-progress of two sculptures. They are 'Head and Hands' by Georgia Wright (above) and 'The Blowing Head' by Mark Fuller (below).

The third sculpture is 'Fish' by Sarah Lankester. 'The Blowing Head' can also be seen behind, as can the recent housing development in North Lane which replaced an old garage complex.

Two of the completed sculptures, with 'Fish' in the foreground, as photographed in September 1992. Along the nearby pathway (right), a wooden plaque named the three carvings and also credited the three sculptors involved.

The completed 'Head and Hands' in September 1992. This sculpture represented Mother Nature holding up her hands in order to protect herself from the Great Storm. Due to the complexity of the idea, the hands were carved separately and then cleverly grafted into place.

'The Blowing Head' represents the full force of the wind on that night, and therefore forms a neat pairing with 'Head and Hands'. Sadly, the sculptures were removed in late 2004. Some say that the wood had rotted away and the sculptures were dangerous, but they had also unfortunately become the target for vandals, and at least one was set on fire.

2

THE CANTERBURY DISTRICT

The author's grandfather poses for the camera with a tree recently toppled by the Great Storm. It once stood on the exposed high ground above the village of Preston and had stood no chance against the unrelenting wind.

Two horse-drawn gypsy caravans used to be parked on the verge near Preston Church. One of them was damaged in the Great Storm, as can be seen in this photograph, taken in late October 1987.

This oast can be found at Preston Court, next to the lovely village church. Both of these buildings suffered storm damage to their roofs, but the oast house came off worst, as this picture clearly testifies. Most of its valuable tiles were completely stripped off by the high winds that night.

The old lane that passes through Bridge on its south side has to negotiate a ford, over which the Nailbourne Stream sometimes passes. This photograph dates from December 1986 and shows quite a low level of water.

In this February 1988 view from the same location, the affects of the Great Storm can clearly be seen. The Nailbourne has also swollen, as it is often want to do, as the stream flows through on its way to Patrixbourne.

For many decades now Reculver, near Herne Bay, has been well known for static caravan holidays. However, in the few years immediately prior to the Great Storm, their numbers had been greatly reduced. Sadly though, the ones that were retained, suffered considerably in the Great Storm, as can be seen in the following four images.

This photograph shows a caravan completely overturned, close to the roadside. In some cases the bodywork has buckled completely; in others, the caravans have been torn to pieces.

These two caravans appear to have become locked together. Sadly, many of these vans had recently been newly purchased to replace older examples.

In the aftermath of the Great Storm, many caravans that had been damaged beyond repair were stripped off their reusable metal cladding and then towed across to the seashore at Reculver. They were then set on fire. Here is one of many caravan 'cremations' that took place in late 1987 and early 1988.

Hillborough can be found between Reculver and Beltinge, to the east of Herne Bay. Being situated on high ground, open to the sea, there was very little protection from the Great Storm. Photographed in late October 1987, this farm outbuilding had collapsed along its entire length (*see* also page 5).

In May 1988, the collapsed barn appeared to be in exactly the same state as it had appeared in the week following the Great Storm. However, the rigid metal framing of its roof supports seem to have saved much of the building's contents from being too badly crushed.

On the opposite side of the road, another building in Hillborough was reduced to rubble. Note the church of St Mary-the-Virgin, which replaced the original Norman foundation at Reculver itself, of which the towers remain today.

This photograph shows a very relaxed approach to the clearing-up process, with much rubble and tottering ruins still in evidence. Today, many of these Hillborough sites have been redeveloped for housing.

This magnificent copper beach tree was photographed in the village of Bekesbourne during the summer of 1986. The picture was taken from the track leading to the church, looking back towards the railway embankment.

Being relatively shallow-rooted, many mature beech trees came to grief during the Great Storm. However, whereas most were uprooted and pushed over by the high winds, this particular specimen sheered off at the base of the trunk, as this dramatic photograph makes clear.

Many beech trees came to grief in the small hours of 16th October 1987. These examples, pictured in January 1988, could be found on the high ground above the villages of Bekesbourne and Patrixbourne.

The site of the lost copper beach tree in early 1988. This is a perfect illustration of the fact that just one lost specimen tree, if impressive enough, can affect a whole area.

Looking down onto the old railway station at Bishopsbourne, on the long-closed Elham Valley Line, in June 1987. The lush foliage of the trees on the embankment either side is so thick that the old station building and surviving platforms can barely be seen.

November 1987 and the situation is very different: a clear view of the old railway station is now possible. Quite apart from the expected seasonal loss of leaves, many of the self-sown trees on the embankment opposite the old station building have been blown down in the Great Storm and now span the old track-bed between platforms.

Just outside the village of Bishopsbourne is Lenhall Farm, where these large evergreen trees have blocked the farm track to all but the most determined of hikers.

Another scene of destruction at Lenhall Farm, photographed in November 1987. Here, the remains of this storage building are being held up by its contents alone. The Elham Valley line once passed beneath the farm, through a tunnel that is still navigable by foot today.

A distant but charming view of Bridge parish church, dedicated to St Peter, photographed just before Christmas in 1986. The mature trees behind the church are along the edge of Bourne Park Road.

Many trees came to grief along the edge of Bourne Park Road, in the vicinity of St Peter's Church at Bridge. Both deciduous and coniferous species were amongst the casualties. This road links the villages of Bridge and Bishopsbourne.

By May 1988, most of the collapsed trees in the area of St Peter's Church, Bridge, had yet to be cleared away. This is understandable for many, if not all of them, had fallen away from the road and into the field beyond.

Another panoramic view of St Peter's Church, as seen from Mill Lane in Bridge. This particular photograph dates from May 1988. As is clear, the church's leafy backdrop is no more and the verge along Bourne Park Road has been extensively denuded of its mature trees.

Bigbury Woods can be found on the highest ground to the south-west of Canterbury, between the villages of Harbledown and Chartham Hatch. A narrow lane runs through these ancient woods, from which many of the following pictures were taken.

A mature evergreen tree has been uprooted in Bigbury Woods, as recorded in this view from May 1988. Part of a row of mature evergreens, it was one of many examples that had collapsed into an area of immature broadleaf coppice beyond.

Another toppled tree close to the winding lane that runs through Bigbury Woods. These woodlands, situated as they are on the highest ground in the area, have always been vulnerable to high winds, and also to the occasional forest fire.

The fallen evergreen trees in Bigbury Woods created some fascinating and unusual photographic studies.

This extremely rural view was taken on the cross-country footpath between Littlebourne and Bekesbourne in March 1987. It begins in the vicinity of Well Chapel, near Littlebourne, and finally emerges through an occupation arch in the railway embankment opposite Bekesbourne Church.

Early November 1987 and it is clear that the overgrown hedgerow, which lined much of this pleasant walk, has been largely destroyed.

Along this rural route could be found two stacks of redundant hop poles; testament to the declining use of hops as a cash crop in Kent. The storm-force winds of 16th October 1987 has set this particular stack at a crazy angle but hasn't actually managed to collapse it.

A contrasting 'after' photograph, captured in March 1988, taken in exactly the same spot as the one at the top of the opposite page. By this time, the clearance process had begun, but the remaining debris had prevented a significant margin of the field from being ploughed, as can be seen here.

Stodmarsh Church on a wet, wintry morning in March 1987. I little realised at the time how many of these beloved East Kent views would change forever later that same year.

Leaving the village and heading towards Wickhambreaux on Sunday, 25th October 1987, I encountered these three hill-top trees that had seemingly fallen over in unison back towards the village.

Another picture taken on the outskirts of Stodmarsh in late October 1987. Framed by these storm-shattered trees is a fine view of Stodmarsh Court: a Grade I listed building with its characteristic Jacobean-style gables.

Stodmarsh Church and village in March 1988. Sadly, only one of the trees seen just a year before still exists. What better illustration could there be to demonstrate the affect of the Great Storm on the Kentish countryside.

Thornden Woods, part of the greater and very ancient Blean Woods, can be found between Canterbury and Herne Bay. This picture, from May 1987, was taken at the beginning of the bridal path that leads from Thornden Woods to West Blean Woods and then onto Herne Common.

The tall row of Evergreen tees seen in the background of the above picture once lined Thornden Wood Road, linking the villages of Tyler Hill and Herne. The Great Storm quickly put paid to these fine specimens.

Elsewhere in Thornden Woods the remains of a woodman's hut could be found, as illustrated in this photograph from April 1988. Its former shape, as an upstanding structure, can only be guessed at.

A contrasting view from the bridal path through Thornden Woods, dating from April 1988. The loss of the roadside row of evergreen trees, as seen on the opposite page, is quite apparent in this later view.

Well Chapel, just outside Littlebourne, is an area dominated by an overgrown plantation of trees, surrounding some natural springs. This is also the point where the Nailbourne stream becomes the more substantial Little Stour River. The area gets its name from a small ruinous chapel that can be seen in some of the following views. This picture was taken in September 1987.

A stile and footpath leading to Well Chapel have been all but buried by the fallen debris from the devastated plantation in this November 1987 view. The mixed trees here were to have been felled in October and replaced by a plantation of ash. However, the Great Storm got there first.

As plans had already been made to fell the plantation, everything was already in place to deal with the aftermath of the Great Storm. Here, only weeks afterwards, the clearing-up process is clearly well advanced. The ruins of Well Chapel can be seen in the background.

The devastated plantation in April 1988. It would appear that there is very little left for the tree surgeons to do, as far as felling is concerned. The area was subsequently replanted with ash trees, as had been planned before the Great Storm intervened.

An extremely high number of outbuildings, both domestic and commercial, were destroyed as a result of the Great Storm. Here, on Sunday, 3rd January 1988, stalwart walkers pass a collapsed building in the tiny hamlet of Nash, near Ash.

On the same Sunday morning walk, which took in Elmstone, Perry, Walmestone and Nash, this small barn was photographed. Note that its load of hay or straw bails is all that is keeping the roof in place.

This collapsed shed could be found just off the road from Canterbury to Bekesbourne and was photographed in January 1988. Such timber-framed structures stood little chance, especially if the integrity of their construction was compromised by a heavy roof.

This elderly, often-repaired shed was found on the lane between Herne Common and West Blean Woods. The old structure has been reduced to so-much firewood.

On a public right-of-way in West Blean Woods, near Herne Common, could once be found this neat rank of coniferous trees lining the track. Opposite, a plantation of silver birch provides an interesting contrast. The photograph was taken in May 1987.

West Blean Woods is a large area of mixed woodland, much of it regularly coppiced. Here, a deciduous tree that had regularly been spared the coppicing process has been snapped by the wind, as if it were no more than a matchstick.

Surrounded by an open area caused by recent coppicing, this exposed tree – ironically retained as a specimen – stood very little chance during the Great Storm. It was photographed as part of a survey of the area in May 1988.

Another view from the public right-of-way, this one dating from April 1988. As a result of the Great Storm, there is now no trace whatsoever of the rank of conifers once found on the right. However, the stand of silver birches appears little affected.

St Andrew's Church, Wickhambreaux, as seen through the bare, wintry trees on the green in 1987.

Sunday, 25th October 1987, and the affects of the Great Storm are apparent; the trees once sheltering the church have been cleared bt high-speed winds. Although the clear-up process had begun, many large trees, trunks and branches still remained where they fell the previous week.

Wickhambreaux Green again and all but one of the mature trees in this area had been blown over. The Rose Inn can be seen in the background.

The author's grandfather stands by the massive root-ball of a blown-over tree, not far from the little house (right) where his mother, Emily Spicer, had been born. The tree had fallen into the grounds of Wickhambreaux House, just visible to the left.

One fairly modest tree, just off Wickhambreaux Green, had fallen right through the roof of a nearby farm outbuilding. On Sunday 25th October, much of its crown remained embedded in the building's shattered tiles and broken rafters.

The bottom half of the same tree, on the opposite side of the road, has clearly demolished this old perimeter wall. The tree's middle section would have been quickly removed so as not to block the main route through the village.

A charming house, called The Court, seen from across Wickhambreaux Green on 25th October 1987. The one remaining tree can be seen on the left, together with the severed limbs of its less fortunate neighbours.

The root-ball of one of the massive trees Wickhambreaux Green that was summarily dispatched in the Great Storm. Beyond is the stunning Wickhambreaux House, which appears to have come through the ordeal without damage.

The brick base of Preston Windmill, near Wingham, photographed on 24th January 1988. The upper timber-constructed portion of this once-impressive smock mill was dismantled in 1959, leaving just this base as a storage shed. Note the old millstones.

The Great Storm ripped off the roof of the old windmill's base and tossed it to one side, like the lid being taken off a biscuit tin. The surviving base was noteworthy in being octagonal on the outside and round inside.

Goodnestone House, set within its impressive walled gardens, seen on a wet day in the summer of 1987. Goodnestone Park surrounds the house and once boasted a fine collection of specimen trees.

The weather was similarly rainy in late February 1988. Sadly, the fine specimen tree immediately adjacent to Goodnestone House had become a victim to the storm and the plantation of Spanish oaks to the right had suffered much damage.

The foot of Sturry Hill on Saturday, 17th October 1987, as seen from the top deck of an East Kent bus, on the Canterbury to Herne Bay route. A day after the Great Storm, and this busy A-road was still reduced to a single carriageway by this toppled tree.

Further up Sturry Hill could be found the buildings of the old Sturry Primary School, which closed in 1986. On first seeing these buildings, in February 1988, it was immediately clear that they had been badly damaged in the Great Storm, with vast areas of roof tiles missing.

On further examination of the closed school buildings, the author discovered that the damage was not just confined to missing roof tiles. A vast tree had plummeted right through the middle of the old school complex, resulting in the sort of devastation seen here.

Before the Great Storm, another use was being sought for these redundant school buildings, but afterwards complete demolition became the only viable option.

Renville Farm, near Bridge, in May 1987. Note the fine specimen tree that provides a splendidly photographic backdrop.

Renville Farm in April 1988, and although the railway bridge and its precious metal sign are still there, they magnificent tree has now gone: another victim of the Great Storm.

This old oak was purposely retained and conserved when the embankment of Bridge bypass was constructed right in its shadow. This photograph from December 1986 was taken from the back road that links the villages of Bridge and Patrixbourne.

The road bridge also carried the bypass over the Nailbourne stream, on whose banks that once mighty oak had thrived. By February 1988, the uprooted and smashed tree could be seen lying next to the stream, its leafy branches no longer softening the harsh lines of the bypass bridge.

A collection of old, twisted and ivy-clad willow trees in the hamlet of Grays, near Herne Bay, growing near the banks of the North Stream. The date is 19th March 1987.

By April 1988, only one tree had remained upright, and the remains of the others still littered the ground where they had fallen in the wake of the Great Storm. The lane in the foreground of both views leads the traveller onto Marshside, Boyden Gate and Chislet.

Another East Kent hamlet, this one being Old Tree near the village of Hoath. Old Tree House is seen here on 29th December 1986, surrounded by a fine collection of trees – including a number of Spanish oaks, which are evergreen.

Old Tree House in March 1988 and many of the trees in its immediate vicinity have disappeared, victims of the Great Storm. The stock of evergreen trees, in particular, seems to have suffered significant loss.

High on a bank above Harbledown bypass, and near to where Palmar's Cross Hill descends from the village of Rough Common, this once mighty evergreen tree had been completely uprooted in the Great Storm.

Another view of the same fallen tree in May 1988. This fine specimen would have originally been planted in the grounds of Hall Place – one of the most noteworthy country houses to be found in and around Harbledown. The bypass cut though its grounds in the mid-1970s.

At the top of Palmar's Cross Hill and much closer to the village of Rough Common, another once mighty tree had been sent crashing to the ground as a result of the Great Storm. Harbledown bypass can just been seen below to the right.

Peter Docherty's bungalow in St Michael's Close, Rough Common, is viewed here from the back garden in the early afternoon of 16th October 1987. The aforementioned collapsed garage is to the left.

Bourne Park is a large area of Capability Brown-style parkland situated between the villages of Bishopsbourne and Bridge. Taken in October 1986, this photograph shows the entrance driveway to Bourne House, flanked by two magnificent cedar of Lebanon trees.

The chalk-flecked root-balls of trees toppled in the Great Storm became a common site from the Bourne Park Road in the aftermath of the Great Storm. This view dates from March 1988.

In March 1988, a willow tree that has fallen into the ornamental lake on Bourne Park struggles to set leaf, with most of its roots now ripped from the ground. Bourne House can be seen in the background on the right.

The grand gateway of the private road to Bourne House is seen here in May 1988. Sadly, the nearer of the two cedar trees now lies smashed on the ground, whereas the furthest example still stands, but is heavily battle-scarred, thanks to the Great Storm.

Other titles published by The History Press

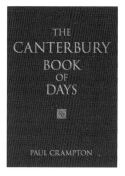

The Canterbury Book of Days

PAUL CRAMPTON

Taking you through the year day by day, *The Canterbury Book of Days* contains a quirky, eccentric, amusing or important event or fact from different periods of history, many of which had a major impact on the religious and political history of England as a whole. Ideal for dipping into, this addictive little book will keep you entertained and informed. Featuring hundreds of snippets of information gleaned from the vaults of Canterbury's archives, it will delight residents and visitors alike.

978 0 7524 5685 0

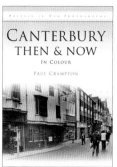

Canterbury Then & Now

PAUL CRAMPTON

In forty-five colourful pairings of archive scenes with modern photography, Paul Crampton captivatingly illustrates the most significant changes that have taken place in Canterbury during the last century, from the redevelopment of the city centre to the evolution of modern transport and fashions, taking the reader on a fascinating journey through the history of Canterbury's streets.

978 0 7524 6296 7

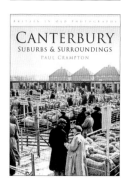

Canterbury: Suburbs & Surroundings

PAUL CRAMPTON

During Roman times, when the city wall first appeared, the areas occupied by today's suburbs were used as burial grounds. From the Saxon period onwards, houses, inns and small businesses appeared along the main approach roads to the city. Through a plethora of previously unpublished photographs, Paul Crampton's book shows the changing shape of these suburbs as they developed during the twentieth century into what we know today.

978 0 7524 5572 3

Kent Folk Tales

TONY COOPER

These traditional stories and local legends have been handed down by storytellers for centuries. As folk tales reveal a lot about the people who invented them, this book provides a link to the ethics and way of life of generations of Kentish people. Herein you will find the intriguing tales of Brave Mary of Mill Hill, King Herla, the Pickpockets of Sturry, the Wantsum Wyrm and the Battle of Sandwich, to name but a few. These captivating stories will be enjoyed by readers time and again.

978 0 7524 5933 2

Visit our website and discover thousands of other History Press books.

www.thehistorypress.co.uk